Praise for *Pairing Paws*

🐾

Michele is one of the best wine educators I've ever had the pleasure of working with. She speaks about wine in such an approachable and fun way. *Pairing Paws* is refreshing to read, both informative and playful. I love that she weaves together snippets about the wineries with the dogs' personalities. What a creative perspective on the wine world!

—Jill Davis, advanced sommelier CMS, winemaker, Cordelette Wine

Michele Gargiulo masterfully breaks down walls and presents a book for imbibers and dog lovers alike that truly is FUN!

—Ross Jackson, sommelier and wine educator

When you are having a 'ruff' day, a great glass of wine and a love of our furry best friends are always there to comfort us. Michele lets us look at our relationship with both in a new way.

—Scott Zoccolillo, advanced sommelier CMS

I have long associated wine with people, places, and music. Michele takes it to another level, as dogs have their own inherent personalities driven by their breeds and owners. Michele's knowledge and expertise are on show for all to see. I thought the photos of the loveable pups were the highlight, then I read the text!

—Hamilton Weaver, sommelier

This book exemplifies not only the importance of wine pairings but also the connections that spark between the glass and the environment that surrounds that glass. Michele perfectly showcases the feeling of a great wine experience, regardless of the specific wine.

—Austin McKenna, sommelier

Pairing wine with anything but food can feel disjointed at best and disingenuous at worst. Michele has managed to walk this line with the incredible grace that is her trademark. This is a genuine showing of passion and expertise in two specialties that can be opaque to most. Every photograph and line of prose shows us something new and exciting through the particular lens of Michele's perspective.

—Jamie Harrison Rubin, sommelier, educator, and podcaster

Pairing Paws

MICHELE GARGIULO

Pairing Paws

Dog Breeds and Their Spirit Wines

Pairing Paws: Dog Breeds and Their Spirit Wines
© 2022 Michele Gargiulo

All rights reserved. No part of this publication may be reproduced in any form or by any electronic or mechanical means, including information storage and retrieval systems, without permission in writing by the publisher, except by a reviewer who may quote brief passages in a review. For information regarding permission, contact the publisher at sommelierstoriespress.com.

Published by Sommelier Stories Press
Philadelphia, PA
Sommelierstoriespress.com

Hardcover ISBN: 979-8-218-01421-6

Edited by Teresa Crumpton of Author Spark and Red to Black Editing
Includes photography by Amanda Jaffe and Carina Romano
Cover and interior design by Liz Schreiter
Produced by Reading List Editorial
ReadingListEditorial.com

This book is dedicated to the man determined to make all my dreams come true: Zakary.

And to all our Furry Friends who kept us sane during the COVID-19 quarantine.

Contents

1	:	Foreword
3	:	Introduction
4	:	African Boerboel
6	:	Akita Inu
8	:	American Bulldog
10	:	American Bully
12	:	American Eskimo
14	:	Australian Shepherd
16	:	Basset Hound
18	:	Beagle
20	:	Belgian Tervuren
22	:	Bernese Mountain Dog
24	:	Bichon Frise
26	:	Blue Heeler
28	:	Border Collie
30	:	Boston Terrier
32	:	Boxer
34	:	Cavalier King Charles Spaniel
36	:	Chihuahua
38	:	Chow Chow
40	:	Cocker Spaniel
42	:	Collie
44	:	Dachshund
46	:	Dalmatian
48	:	Doberman Pinscher
50	:	English Bulldog
52	:	English Mastiff
54	:	English Springer Spaniel
56	:	Fox Terrier
58	:	French Bulldog
60	:	German Shepherd
62	:	German Shorthaired Pointer
64	:	Golden Retriever
66	:	Great Dane
68	:	Great Pyrenees
70	:	Greyhound
72	:	Havanese
74	:	Irish Setter
76	:	Jack Russell Terrier
78	:	Labrador Retriever
80	:	Maltese
82	:	Papillon
84	:	Pit Bull
86	:	Pomeranian
88	:	Poodle
90	:	Pug
92	:	Rottweiler
94	:	Saint Bernard
96	:	Schnauzer
98	:	Scottish Terrier
100	:	Shetland Sheepdog
102	:	Shiba Inu
104	:	Shih Tzu
106	:	Siberian Husky
108	:	Silky Terrier
110	:	Welsh Corgi
112	:	Welsh Terrier
114	:	West Highland Terrier
116	:	Yorkshire Terrier
119	:	Acknowledgments
121	:	About the Author

Foreword

BY BRANDON FORD

For my family and me, dogs are as important as any other aspect of life, including wine. I work as a beverage director for a medium-sized restaurant group, selecting, educating, and working with wine and spirits for all our locations. Wine is integrated into our family just as much as Tessa (a German shepherd and Siberian husky mix) and Lily (our neurotic Labrador rescue) are. I look back and see pictures of Foster, my oldest son, holding a champagne flute filled with orange juice when he's three. Arlo, my youngest son, attempting to pick out a bottle of wine from our basement. Wine is never the focal point of these family pictures, yet, it always seems to be there, an accompaniment to the joy that is frozen in time.

At times, some of that joy of wine gets lost for me. It gets lost when wine snobbery is allowed to take hold around me. It gets lost when I read about scandal after scandal in corporate America, including the #metoo movement, which encompasses all businesses, including much of the wine industry. It gets lost when I read and hear personal anecdotes about being excluded from this elite group of wine insiders.

But it doesn't have to be this way. Those family pictures remind me of that. Those family pictures remind me that wine is not only paired with food, but it's paired with occasions, with personalities, with emotions, and yes, even with dogs. Trust me when I say that Lily would pair with a high-energy, laser-focused Grosses Gewächs Riesling, and Tessa, well, Tessa pairs well with an exuberant, meaty, Châteauneuf-du-Pape. Meet them, and you'll understand.

—Brandon Ford,
Advanced Sommelier, CMS-Americas
Beverage Director

Introduction

Ever wonder which wine to pair with something you have *no intention* of eating? Winemaking is an art form Yes, art! It's a type of art that survives time in a way most things cannot: it is still living and growing.

If you moseyed into the Louvre, stepped up, and licked the Mona Lisa, you would certainly get into trouble and you might be offered a lovely test of your sobriety—or your sanity. The Mona Lisa, like most art, is meant to be experienced with only one or two of your senses.

But wine you can see, taste, and smell. At one point before they found their way into the bottle in front of you, those grapes were growing in the sunlight against great odds. Some winemakers ply their art amid wars or political unrest; others brave the natural elements like wind, hail, mold, snow, fire, hurricanes, and earthquakes.

Those grapes could have been growing long before you were born, before you were little more than a haploid somewhere. Like other artists, the winemaker had a vision they brought to life, capturing the sunlight, turning it into living poetry that continues to age and develop with time.

While I love traditional wine-pairing books—and as a sommelier, I am passionate about food and wine—something has been missing from the wine world, and that is fun! I have taken the time to make some unusual, inedible (hopefully, anyway) pairings to a beverage or two. This book explores how to pair the personality and soul of different wines with well-known dog breeds. From pairing a Yorkshire terrier with Trimbach's Clos Ste-Hune to pairing a Siberian husky with Inniskillin Cabernet Franc Icewine, this book traverses the complex world of wine to make it as fun as a freshly cracked bottle of champagne!

African Boerboel

Atlas & Nyah

The African Boerboel Is Friendly, but Stubborn

Originally bred in South Africa, the African Boerboel is a large mastiff breed. Often used as a homestead guardian or as a working farm dog, this breed can be slightly difficult to train.

Paired with our African Boerboel, we have Small Vines Estate Cuvée. This is a deep, brooding expression of Pinot Noir that comes from the family-run operation of Paul and Kathryn Sloan, whose children assist in the vineyards. With a smaller production run, this wine ages with grace and elegance yet still tastes refined in its youth. This grape varietal is among the oldest of those still being planted today, so there are many different clones of this grape for winemakers to choose from according to which works best for them.

Pinot Noir is one of the most difficult grapes to grow well—almost as stubborn as our friend the African Boerboel. Both the grape and the pup are tough and stubborn, yet elegant and beautiful when given the appropriate care and attention. Densely planted vines have resulted in deeply concentrated flavors of wild porcini mushrooms, grilled bacon, and ripe red cherry that swirl up out of the glass at you. Firm yet supple tannins are balanced by the bright and noticeable acidity.

I recommend enjoying this wine with the Shroom Burger from Shake Shack while you sit on a park bench with your pooch looking lovingly up at you, waiting patiently for some cheese to drip onto your lap.

The Akita Inu Is Large and Highly Alert

Japanese in origin, the Akita, according to legend, was bred to hunt the Yezo bear (Japan's largest land animal, weighing up to 1,100 pounds!), and they are still used to hunt large boar and elk to this day. Very loyal and fearless, these dogs are considered good luck.

Paired with this pup is a Hakkaisan Sparkling "AWA" Sake. Sake is a rice wine made primarily in Japan, and Hakkaisan is made from the rice varietals Gohyakumangoku and Yamada Nishiki, believed to be the most suitable for sake.

Hakkaisan carefully selects the location and the growers of their rice for each batch of this wine. Their traditional production methods and strictly selected ingredients produce some of the best-quality sake in the world—just as dignified as the noble Akita.

This particular wine is elegant, clean, and crisp, with a hint of sweetness on the finish. Amid the aromas of ripe white peaches and grilled tangerines, this wine whispers of dried jasmine blossoms and freshly fallen snow. This gently sparkling sake is sure to make you as alert as your Akita. The Sake School of America says sake gives one "natural energy."

I recommend enjoying the wine chilled while catching snowflakes on your tongue, sitting by a warm fire with one hand gently stroking your Akita's scruff.

The American Bulldog Is Confident and Dominant, yet Gentle

*S*hockingly enough, the American bulldog originates from America! These easily trained dogs are often used for hunting, as stock dogs, and on farms where they might be found hard at work chasing away feral pigs.

Paired with our American bulldog, we have a Cheval des Andes Malbec blend from Argentina. Malbec is a grape variety that was grown extensively in Bordeaux before the phylloxera epidemic came through Europe in the late 1800s. These pesky root lice made it impossible for the native grapes to remain on their own rootstock, resulting in a mass effort to graft American rootstock to European tops. But the malbec grape did not graft well and was disowned by most Bordeaux growers.

In Argentina, French winemaker Pierre Lurton dreamed of restoring malbec to its former glory. This is a vibrant and intense wine, with a unique blend. The different grape varieties come together in a symphony, as well-balanced as the majestic American bulldog itself.

Created by the masterminds behind Cheval Blanc, this is a high-quality wine grown in the best area of Mendoza. The malbec dominates (like our bulldog) the flavor profile, with blueberries, black cherries, leather, and tobacco reigning supreme, while the Cabernet Sauvignon and petit verdot take a backseat with their flaky fig pastry and dark-chocolate-covered espresso beans. Rounded yet firm tannins mimic the gentle but confident attitude of the American bulldog.

I recommend enjoying this malbec blend with figs wrapped in bacon while binge-watching *The Office* and playing with a squeaky stuffed squirrel toy with your pal.

American Bully

Honeyboy

The American Bully Is Affectionate and Gentle

With a name that couldn't be more opposite their personality, American bullies are fun-loving and intelligent. These dogs are shorter and squatter than their pit bull relatives, but they can be every bit as social.

Fiercely loyal and protective of their family, these dogs do require early training to curb any aggressiveness. But this breed is known for being extremely patient with children, and they love to buddy up with their families' youngest members.

Paired with the American bully, we have Tenuta Santa Maria's Pragal from Verona. A delightful blend of corvina, merlot, and Syrah gives this wine a rich complexity and astonishing length. Some of the grapes have been allowed to dry, which concentrates the flavors and intensifies the palate.

Both the wine and the dog come from distinguished backgrounds, the wines from the Bertani family. Firm yet silky and plush with rounded tannins, the body of this wine mimics the rounded and muscular body of the bully.

Raspberry jam, dried violet petals, and Cuban cigars burst to life on the nose. The palate brings baking spices, black cherry, and freshly crushed black peppercorns into the mix as well. This wine matches the bully's patience as it is delicious and drinkable when young, but can age for many years to come.

I recommend enjoying this wine on a wooden deck while eating beef carpaccio, heavy on the horseradish, as your American bully stands guard against any intrepid bird that might come swooping down at you.

The American Eskimo Is Bright, Lively, and Easy to Love

The "eskie" originated in Germany, where they were bred to guard people's homes. They migrated their way to the United States and have been developed into the American Eskimo breed we know and love today: smaller in size than the original German breed, but high in activity levels and alertness, and easy to train.

Paired with this furry friend, we have Desparada's Fragment, a sauvignon blanc from California. This amphora-aged wine has a smooth and refreshing texture to it, coating the glass with a mineral quality as obvious as the American Eskimo's beautiful fur.

Vailia From is the brilliant female winemaker behind the bottle. With a personality just as loveable as the American Eskimo's, she was told early in her career by the TTB that her labels (which feature sketches of naked women) were inappropriate. She complied with regulations by creating composite sketches of the same nudes in the shape of clothing to introduce a little modesty. If you look closely at the labels, you can tell her women are actually wearing other women!

Bright, lively, and easy to love, this sauvignon blanc has a similar personality to our canine companion: happy, yet well-balanced. Bright ruby grapefruit, freshly cut grass, and kumquat resonate on the palate of this wine. Limestone lingers on the tantalizingly long finish, and visions of standing on a cliff overlooking the sea come to mind.

I recommend you enjoy the wine with PopCorners sea salt chips after doing some outdoor yoga with your American Eskimo.

Australian Shepherd

🐾

Stella Blue & Mac

The Australian Shepherd Is Active and Approachable for All Ages

This breed does not actually originate from Australia, but from the United States. With high intelligence and high energy, the Australian shepherd makes a great family dog.

These are smart working dogs with strong herding and guarding instincts. They are loyal companions and have the stamina to work all day. They have a well-balanced medium size, completely in proportion, with coloring that offers variety and individuality.

The Australian shepherd is paired with Elements Syrah, grown in the Finger Lakes of New York. Made by master sommelier Christopher Bates, this wine exudes freshly cracked black pepper, crushed violets, red and black forest fruits, and savory, smoky nuance.

The deep, earthy backbone of this wine perfectly parallels the strong, centered backbone of our working dog. With high energy in the glass, this wine is definitely as intellectually stimulating as our Australian shepherd. While this wine is not yet as well-known as our dog, it is from a vastly underestimated region.

It is found to be low in alcohol, high in acid, and intensely mineral, made lean by the acid yet structured by the tannins. Approachably priced, Elements Syrah is accessible to all wine drinkers. Almost as appreciable as our shepherd, and just as lively.

I recommend enjoying the wine with grilled pork-belly shish kabobs, pulled off the grill in your backyard while tossing bites to your Australian shepherd.

The Basset Hound Has Big-Dog Strength and Stamina

French in origin, this short-legged hound dog has a truly astounding sense of smell. This hunting dog has been around for a long time. Bassets are famous for their large heads, extremely long ears, sad eyes, and wrinkled brows, which make them easy to feature in cartoons. Built more for endurance than speed, the basset moves at a deliberate, yet slow and effortless pace.

Paired with our hound dog is Matthiasson Pinot Meunier. A stunning wine brought to life in one of the first certified-organic vineyards in Napa, California, this wine has aromatics to last for days. Steve and Jill Matthiasson are farmers through and through, trying to maximize the expressiveness of their wines with as little human intervention as possible.

Bright raspberry, orange zest, pomegranate, dried jasmine, and wet white pebbles dominate the palate. As the name implies, this grape originated from our pooch's country of origin, France. Meunier, best known for its use as a blending grape in Champagne, is among the least well-known offshoots of Pinot Noir, lending it a certain romantic sadness to match the basset hound's looks. This wine is highly aromatic, which our basset hound, with its incredible sense of smell, can really appreciate.

I recommend enjoying this wine with Craisins, sitting on the floor, with your basset hound between your legs.

Beagle

🐾 Tommy

The Beagle Is Loving and Loveable

United Kingdom-bred, these intelligent pups are used to hunt hare and small game. They have a wonderful sense of smell and make great family dogs. Often described as "intensely happy" by their fans, beagles are exuberant and companionable. The beagle is consistently one of the top-rated dog breeds in America by the American Kennel Club. These are curious, clever, and energetic hounds who require plenty of playtime.

Paired with this popular pup is Domaine Leflaive Bourgogne Blanc, a spectacular wine made by one of the most respected winemakers in Burgundy. Biodynamically grown, these grapes are always picked by hand, and their wines always stand out in a lineup of top Burgundy producers.

Joseph Leflaive was originally an engineer who helped to create the first French submarine. He returned home from war to take over his family vines and replace those destroyed by phylloxera infestations. After the 1920s, Leflaive created his own label.

Chardonnay is an incredibly versatile grape, and it is one of the most popular grown in the world today. The expression is lean and regal, with jasmine, chamomile, grilled almonds, and fresh juicy peaches on the nose. The palate is striking, with lemon peel and wet rocks rounding out the complexity.

Both the wine and the dog are highly sought-after companions. The aromas of this wine pair beautifully with the loving, lively characteristics of the beagle. I recommend enjoying this wine with lightly smoked trout while sitting on white pebbles at the side of a trickling stream, tossing a stick for your beagle friend to fetch.

The Belgian Tervuren Is an Awesome Sniffer and Very Sensitive

Used frequently as a drug- and bomb-detecting breed, these classic Belgian herd dogs are highly intelligent, easy to train, and loyal. They are also highly empathetic, which has led to them often being found as therapy dogs and service heroes. This breed takes real delight in their ability to master any task, and owners say a mischievous sense of humor is at work whenever Tervurens outsmart their beloved humans.

Paired with our Belgian Tervuren, we have Six Hats Chenin Blanc from the Western Cape of South Africa. This heroic winemaker subscribes to the principles of the Fair Trade movement, making sure that everyone who has anything to do with creating this great wine is paid a fair, livable wage. This shows the Six Hats group is as loyal to its workers as the Belgian Tervuren is to its owners.

Harvested early in the mornings before the sun has risen to retain the delicate floral aromatics, this wine is created using only the free-run juices. This means the grapes are never squeezed—the gentle pressure of grape on top of grape allows the juice to run freely. This delicate process ensures that the juice is of the highest quality, with no bitter notes infused via seeds, stems, or skins.

Clean and crisp, with floral notes like orange blossom, jasmine, ginger, and pineapple coming through on the nose, this wine is as gorgeous on the palate as the stunning coat is on the Belgian Tervuren. Tangerine and minerality are the lingering components on the finish. I recommend enjoying this wine with a classic tuna and avocado roll while holding paws with your loyal little friend.

Bernese Mountain Dog

Nigel

The Bernese Mountain Dog Is Affectionate and Powerful

Originally bred as farm dogs in the mountains of Switzerland, Bernese mountain dogs are beautiful, majestic, and intelligent friends. They are easy to train, calm, and friendly. Large, powerful, and strong, the Bernese mountain dog is also striking in appearance and has a kind, affectionate nature. Berners are generally tranquil but are always up for a wild frolic with their owners.

Paired with this strong dog, we have Vega Sicilia Unico. While the Bernese mountain dog is without equal when it comes to strength and kindness, this majestic bottle is considered by many to be the gold standard of Spanish wine, made from the tempranillo grape blended with Cabernet Sauvignon.

Before it is bottled, it is aged in oak for a minimum of ten years. The result is an undeniably smooth and bold yet serene wine. Due to the lengthy aging process, this wine is ready to drink upon purchase but grows exponentially more delicious with each passing year. Waiting to open it might be a challenge, but it will be worth it, even if the delay is just a few more years.

Created with native yeast, this wild fermented wine really takes on the taste of the land it is grown on, picking up leather, tobacco, violets, coffee, and allspice. Toffee and dried herbs linger on the lasting finish. Just like the Bernese mountain dog, there are few people who do not love this wine after meeting it. Few wines can hold a candle to this one—it tends to stand out in even the most remarkable of wine lineups. I recommend enjoying this wine with lamb lollipops garnished with rosemary, making sure to share a bite or two with your Bernese mountain dog.

The Bichon Frise Is Chipper and Intelligent

The bichon frise is French in origin but has been used by the Spanish as sailing dogs. They are also very popular with the Italian royal family. They have a little less awareness of their surroundings than other breeds. Their fur is white and luscious, and they can be somewhat chatty. Since the beginning of this breed, these happy-go-lucky canines have relied on charm, good looks, and intelligence to remain relevant in a world full of small dog breeds.

Paired with the bichon frise is Field Recordings Wonderwall Chardonnay from Edna Valley. Andrew Jones does a wonderful job taming the wild world of Chardonnay in this oak-loving region. Wonderwall sources their grapes from extreme coastal climates, allowing their Chardonnay to keep a bright acidity.

Golden fruit, a luscious palate and fragrance, enough oak to lift and enhance a lovely, balanced acidity, and a crisp, extremely long-lasting finish make this an easy drinking wine. If dogs could consume wine (they can't, please don't give your dog wine!), I have no doubt the bichon frise would spend its days lounging on the porch, lapping up this wine, occasionally taking a break to drunkenly chase away audacious squirrels.

The style is rich (like these royal canines) and lavish. The wine is almost as charming as the bichon frise itself and is sure to be a party pleaser. I recommend enjoying the wine with grilled prawns on your front porch, listening to jazz music while keeping your pup on a leash in case a squirrel happens by (or a leaf gets blown on the wind).

The Blue Heeler Is Powerful and Energetic

Also known as the Australian cattle dog, the blue heeler is related to the wild dingo. This dog is powerful and able to herd large farm animals such as cattle. Their nickname "heeler" comes from their tendency to nip at the heels of cows.

Considered a "Velcro" dog, the heeler will bond intensely with one person and follow them around. Their endless energy and smooth gait make them excellent running partners, and given their intelligence, they often outsmart their owners.

Paired with our powerful pup, we have Continuum Estate's Novicium. Created by the Mondavi family, this legendary winery overlooks Napa Valley from Pritchard Hill. Robert Mondavi spent the last few years of his life looking for the perfect vineyard to create amazing masterpieces in. The year they finally closed on this stunning property was the same year he died, leaving his children and grandchildren behind to continue his dream of an estate wine.

This wine is a blend of all the grape varieties that cling to each other—like the blue heeler! Each vintage varies on its *cépage*, but they use primarily Cabernet Sauvignon, Cabernet Franc, merlot, and petit verdot. Strong as the blue heeler, this wine is structured well, with full, angular tannins. Created using their youthful vines (that are almost as energetic as the blue heeler), this wine is sold only direct from the winery.

Dark-red cherry and plum dance gracefully out of the glass. Mocha, spice, and licorice make an appearance on the palate, rounding out the complexity and bringing this beautiful wine to life. I recommend enjoying this wine with a Slim Jim and tossing tasty meat treats to your blue heeler.

Border Collie

Milo

The Border Collie Is Sensitive and Athletic

The border collie is an athletic, medium-sized dog from the United Kingdom. Developed for sheep herding, they are still frequently used in this capacity. Overall, this dog appears muscular, but lean and athletic. They can be sensitive and do not like extreme temperatures.

Paired with our border collie, we have Domaine Dujac Echezeaux. Jacques Seysses started the vineyard in 1967 after purchasing it from Domaine Graillet. Today, they use organic and biodynamic farming practices, keeping the wines honest to their place of origin.

Echezeaux is one of the most recognizable Grand Cru vineyards of Burgundy, producing wines with more structure than some of their neighbors. Similar to the sensitive border collie, Pinot Noir is a notoriously fickle grape varietal. It does not like less than perfect growing conditions, and it is incredibly difficult to vinify correctly.

Domaine Dujac is well known for the stunning expressions and longevity of their Pinot Noir. Slightly spicy yet reassuringly floral on the nose, this wine gently beckons you in with dusty chocolate aromas. The palate is brought to life by juicy cherry, dried cranberry, and a refreshing whisper of earth.

Tantalizingly delicious, this wine can absolutely be drunk in its youth or put down to relax for a few years. As lean as the athletic pup, this wine is the essence of the border collie in a few sips. I recommend enjoying this wine with chicken fingers while watching your border collie jump through hoops.

Boston Terrier

🐾
Hope

The Boston Terrier Is Exceedingly Bright

Their tuxedo-looking appearance has gained the Boston terrier the nickname of the "American gentleman." Excelling in sport, these dogs are very outgoing and make fine therapy dogs. However, if they are not trained when they are young, they can be yappy. Boston terriers are sturdy but portable, people-loving, and always up for a brisk (even if short) walk around the park.

Paired with this fancy little gentleman (or lady), we have Pol Roger champagne. One of the very few luxury champagne houses still family-owned today, it screams quality with every sip. Aged to perfection, this wine spends anywhere from two to three times longer in the cellar (pre-disgorgement) than the requirements of champagne dictate.

This was the champagne served at the royal wedding between Prince Harry of Wales and Princess Meghan Markle, and it has long been considered the "gentleman's champagne." Like most champagnes, this is a blend of Chardonnay, Pinot Noir, and meunier grapes. It is released after a minimum of four years of aging in the cellars, which lends a lovely toasted note to the wine.

The aroma is one dominated by fruit: pears, mango, and quince, with underlying notes of freshly baked brioche. The palate is a symphony of minerality and beeswax, brought to crescendo with cardamom and crushed shells. The extended and slow maturation time on the lees really imparts a wholesome mouthfeel, rich and creamy. Just as fancy as your Boston terrier, this wine will make you feel ready for a sophisticated evening. I recommend enjoying this delicious wine with French fries while wearing your tuxedo or cocktail gown.

The Boxer Is Upbeat and Undeniably Playful

German in descent, boxers are frequently found among the top ten most popular dog breeds in America. These muscular dogs were originally used for large-game hunting; now they are used in search-and-rescue efforts with law enforcement and as therapy dogs. More patient than most, this is a fiercely loyal and protective breed.

Paired with our boxer, we have Arrepiado Velho Tradição Tinto from Alentejo, Portugal. Marta and Antonio offer a stunning demonstration of indigenous grapes that really shine when grown with love and care. One hundred percent Touriga Nacional, this wine is truly remarkable with its muscular yet refined structure.

Not as well-known as the boxer, this wine is nonetheless a real crowd pleaser. If you are a fan of Cabernet Sauvignon, this wine is sure to impress you, and at a shockingly lower price point. This grape exudes notes of chocolate-covered blackberries, rose petals, and fresh violets. The palate is incredibly complex, with notes of rosemary, coffee, and salted caramel intermingling with the fruit characteristics.

Not only is the juice a work of art, but the labels are all designed by Marta, and you'd be hard-pressed to find a prettier bottle of wine. This wine is strong enough to last for years—you might need to borrow some patience from your boxer to resist drinking it in its youth. I recommend enjoying this wine with Bagel Bites (preferably with pepperoni) while trying to hide all the squeaky toys from your boxer pal.

Cavalier King Charles Spaniel

Pip & Louie

The Cavalier King Charles Spaniel Is Friendly and Sweet

Originally, these puppers were bred in the United Kingdom. This obedient dog breed does not make for a good watchdogs due to their overly enthusiastic personalities, but they are cuddly and loveable and terrific therapy dogs.

The Cavalier's grace is almost regal. Their excessive patience and gorgeous coats mark them as nobility of the dog world. The Cavalier draws you in with its face: a sweet, gentle, melting expression from large, round eyes is a breed hallmark.

Paired with our Cavalier King Charles spaniel is Folkway Deviator Semillon. A stunning wine with gorgeous texture, this is the perfect pairing for our loveable and easygoing pooch. Fig, honey, fresh jasmine, lilies, and tarragon with a crunchy texture make this wine special.

Semillon is a grape varietal rarely grown in the United States, and it is typically used as a blending grape (just like Cavalier King Charles spaniels have many offshoots and are frequently bred with other dogs). But on its own, if conditions are optimal, this wine can hit a level of complexity.

Well established in Bordeaux, it is typically used in white blends or dessert wines. Australia (Hunter Valley) is also giving the Bordelaise a run for its money as they create some truly lip-smacking expressions of this grape. The Semillon is strong enough to stand on its own feet and is almost as elegant and regal as the Cavalier. I recommend enjoying this wine with a Connecticut-style lobster roll (warm with butter) while playing tug of war with your Cavalier King Charles spaniel.

The Chihuahua Is Compact and Confident

One of the oldest dog breeds in the Americas, the Chihuahua originated in Mexico. You can label it the "tiny dog with huge personality." Because they can be yappy, it is important to socialize them early to avoid developing aggressive tendencies. Compact and excessively confident, Chihuahuas are best as city pets. Due to their smaller stature, they are not ideal for households with children, and they will absolutely need a sweater in colder weather. Still, Chihuahuas are adaptable. However, their preferred state of being is resting on their owners' laps.

Paired with our Chihuahua, we have Hacienda La Lomita's Pagano, grown in Valle de Guadalupe in Baja, Mexico. Owner Fernando Pérez-Castro has created a stunning winery that showcases local artists. It is definitely worth the visit if you are in the area. Organically grown grapes worked by hand boost this wine's sustainability and lower the winery's carbon footprint. This wine has flown under the radar for too long.

Pure grenache, this wine has some body to it, but is on the lighter side (similar to our little Chihuahua friend). Grenache can be easily overblown if it is not grown correctly. As is, this wine is almost aggressively aromatic, with stunning violets, lavenders, and ripe cherries on the nose. The palate is not as big as its aromatic bark, with soft and silky tannins. This is a little-known winery in a region that is growing quickly, with vintners moving here from around the world to enjoy the Baja soil. I recommend enjoying this wine with slow-roasted chicken, potatoes, carrots, and tomatoes, and don't forget to share with your tiny friend!

Chow Chow

🐾 Leo

The Chow Chow Is Refined and Dignified

Chinese in origin, independent and powerful, puffy chow chows are easily recognized. Genetic testing puts this as one of the most ancient dog breeds. Aloof by nature, the chow chow does not love other dogs, and they will take a while to warm up to new humans.

Chows have a reputation for being the cleanest of dogs. They are quick to housebreak and have little doggy odor.

Paired with these particular dogs is Royal Tokaji Essencia, which comes from one of the oldest wine regions on the planet, in line with this ancient breed. This wine is one of the sweetest available, and it does not appeal to a majority of the dessert-skipping population (much like the majority of people do not appeal to the chow). With the grapes harvested entirely by hand and the wine created in one of the most labor-intensive methods, with minimal chemical intervention in the vineyards, these vintages take years before they are released.

Remarkable on the nose and intense on the palate, this wine boasts juicy white peaches, candied ginger, dried apricot, and a pleasant lingering flavor of Earl Grey tea. If you think you are not a fan of dessert wines, please, try this one. It is refreshingly acidic and never cloying in its sweetness; rather, it is perfectly balanced. This wine is sunshine captured in liquid form. If you cannot get your hands on this particular wine, I'd suggest trying their 6 Puttonyos. I recommend enjoying this wine with torched foie gras and toasted bread at a fancy dinner party while sneaking your chow bites of food under the table in an attempt to get it to like you.

The Cocker Spaniel Is Bright and Sensitive

The cocker spaniel has origins in Spain and the United Kingdom. Happy in nature and always sweet, this breed was originally used as a bird-hunting dog. Cocker spaniels might try to chase every squirrel they see, but in general, they make wonderful family dogs.

Cockers are eager playmates for kids, too, and they do not shy away from children the way some other smaller dogs do. They're easily trained as companions for athletes and they are happy to run and exercise. And they're sized perfectly to be portable but are also built to be sporty.

Paired with our happy-go-lucky friend is Dr. Loosen Blue Slate Kabinett Riesling. This wine works to capture the essence of Mosel Riesling from old vines spread throughout the estate's six Grand Cru vineyard sites. The Loosen family, currently headed by Ernst Loosen, has owned their vineyards for more than 200 years.

This wine has just a hint of sweetness, but is so complex that even people who insist they do not like sweet wines are sure to enjoy the high-toned, spicy aromas of baked apple, peach cobbler, minerals, and smoky slate on the nose. Intense and focused on the palate with flavors of white peach, green apple, key lime pie, and shimmering wet stone, the volcanic and slate-filled soil is present on the finish with a refreshing lingering minerality. Both this wine and the cocker spaniel are sure to make you smile. I recommend enjoying this wine with smoked ham and cheese while watching romantic comedies and doing your best to avoid the begging gaze of your little furry friend.

Collie

🐾
Bowie

The Collie Is Sensitive and Intelligent

Scottish in origin, these beautiful dogs were originally sheep herders. Highly intelligent and easily trained, they do not like loud noises or small spaces. They are definitely well suited to large, outdoor areas where they can roam. Well known lovers of little children, these are good family dogs.

Paired with this free-ranging pal is Teutonic Whole Cluster pinot noir. These stunning wines are created in Oregon but are heavily influenced by German varietals. The winemaker, Barnaby, insists upon growing his grapes in vineyards that are only dry-farmed and have vines twenty years of age or older, planted on higher-elevation sites to retain their freshness and acidity.

For such an open-space-loving dog, we had to choose a wine that also loves air. This whole-cluster, naturally fermented wine is made in tanks with space for a carbon dioxide layer on top—air is literally part of the winemaking process for this treat. Ripe blueberry, cherry, and blackberry notes sing to life on the nose; clove and cola plus a green note like tough grass being cut come to life on the palate. With soft and delicate tannins, there is still a lovely structure to this wine. Blueberry and cherry with clove confirm the aromatics, while green apple and clean potting soil shimmer into the lingering finish.

Similar to the sensitive collie, this wine (because of its fermentation process) is sensitive to loud noises and you should avoid shaking the bottle too much. I recommend enjoying the wine with pancetta, apple, and pecan puffs while watching your collie roam around outside, sniffing leaf after leaf.

The Dachshund Is Clever and Lively

The adorable dachshund has a host of nicknames: "wiener dog," "hot dog," "sausage dog." Whatever you call it, this German dog with short little legs and a long body was originally used to hunt badgers (translated, their name means badger dog) and other dangerous prey.

Dachshunds aren't built for distance running, leaping, or swimming, but they are adventurous and like to try new things. Intelligent and alert, with a deep bark, they make great watchdogs. Courageous, this breed can be brave to the point of recklessness and a bit stubborn, but their delightful nature and distinctive look is well-known and loved.

Paired with this lively little fellow is Marcel Lapierre Morgon. Morgon is one of the crus of Beaujolais, made with gamay noir. This wine strives to be as natural as possible, with no pesticides, herbicides, or fertilizers added in the field to these forty-year-old vines, and no sulfur or yeast added during the winemaking process. Marcel Lapierre is one of the revolutionary men who wanted to bring back the old ways of making Beaujolais, and he has been joined in his beliefs by his son Mathieu and daughter Camille, who now use biodynamics in their vineyards.

This is a truly delicious wine, wild and attractive as our brave dachshund. Bright and fleshy fruit impart a gorgeous ruby coloring in the glass. The wine has ripe strawberry aromas, leading to a super juicy and deep-set impression. The palate carries a lithe, juicy, and very energetic array of super-expressive fruit and a hint of savory complexity that just starts on the finish. Do not mistake this wine for the simple Beaujolais Nouveau wines that are released every year: this bottle has a much more impressive structure and flavor. I recommend enjoying the wine with a hot dog, of course!

The Dalmatian Is Powerful and Athletic

Croatian in origin, well-known and easily recognized by their spots, dalmatians are used in firehouses and as rescue dogs. They were created as a breed to guard carriages and the horses that ran them. Dalmatians are muscular and built for distance running; the powerful rear of this animal provides the drive behind their smooth stride.

Paired with the dalmatian, we have Bruno Clair Marsannay rosé. This wine actually saved the appellation of Marsannay from being declassified when the region had fallen out of style, outshined by its southern neighbors. Bruno Clair decided to take his Pinot Noir and make a rosé out of it, lightly pressing his grapes to achieve a pleasant pink hue. He then made the wine fashionable by marketing it to the town of Dijon. Without this wine, the wines of Marsannay would not exist today.

The dalmatian and this wine are both pretty heroic. With stunning aromatics, this wine has floral notes such as rose petals and lavender singing to be heard. Organically grown (but not certified as such), these vineyards are tended by one of the most respected producers in Burgundy, with an eye for detail.

Raspberry and pomegranate come to life on the palate, and clean, crisp minerality steals the show on the finish. Both the wine and the dog can go the distance, as these rosés are some of the longest lasting out there. I recommend enjoying the wine with charcoal-grilled chicken while keeping your spotted friend nearby—just in case some food drops to the ground.

Doberman Pinscher

Devon

The Doberman Pinscher Is Strong and Alert

Considered the most effective guard dog in the world, the Doberman pinscher is German in origin. This magnificent breed is often used in search-and-rescue operations. The man who bred these dogs, a tax collector named Louis Dobermann, wanted the muscle to back up his career. A highly trained Doberman on patrol would absolutely deter all but the most foolish of intruders.

Paired with our firm and brave dog, we have Hentley Farm's Beast. Big, bold, and muscular, this wine tastes as powerful as the Doberman is. The wine was established by Keith and Alison Hentschke with the goal of showcasing single-estate wines from Barossa Valley. Andrew Quin is the current winemaker, and he does an incredible job extracting every ounce of flavor from these grapes.

Opulent, complex, and rich is the way this cuvée of Shiraz from Australia is made. Shiraz is the same grape as the French syrah, but when made in this style from this area of the world, the wine tends to be known as Shiraz.

Not as fruity as some of these wines can be, this one is all about the rich freshly ground pepper, nutmeg, cinnamon, violets, and meatiness. The wine brings to mind walking into a recently finished wooden barn, where the wood is still smelling new and the earth was recently overturned, but no animal smells have yet taken residence.

The structure and body of this wine mimic the sinewy form of the Doberman. I recommend enjoying this decadent wine with some teriyaki beef jerky right before robbing a bank—make sure to share the tasty snack with your partner in crime, the Doberman.

English Bulldog

Gracie Belle

The English Bulldog Is Loving and Gentle

The English bulldog, a British-bred dog, is adored around the world. The breed was originally used for bull-baiting. Sluggish and slow, these pups prefer to sit on the couch with their owners, but they do require some exercise to stay healthy and trim.

It's better to spend hot summer days in an air-conditioned room, as a bulldog's short snout can make excessive heat and humidity difficult for this pup. If it is not too hot out, however, our bulldog enjoys brisk walks.

Paired with our English bulldog, we have the slow-fermenting Barbera della Stoppa from Emilia-Romagna, Italy. The wine is unfined, unfiltered, and no sulfites are added. No yeast is added either; only the wild yeasts captured in the air are used to create this showpiece, so maceration time is extended to more than thirty days. This is far out of the norm and significantly slower than the vast majority of red wines (like our sluggish bulldog!).

Founded more than a century ago, the vineyards grow alongside the Trebbiola Valley. Sauteed mushrooms, dried forest floor, sour red cherries, and a kiss of oak tantalize your nose. Dark chocolate bursting with juicy blackberries join a hint of new leather on the palate.

Just as well loved as the bulldog, Barbera is what most of the winemakers and vineyard workers drink in the fields. There is a saying that it takes a lot of barbera to make Barolo. I recommend enjoying this wine with Domino's pizza while standing over the kitchen counter, avoiding eye contact with your bulldog.

English Mastiff

Herkules

The English Mastiff Has a Large Bark, but Not So Much Bite

Another ancient breed, the English mastiff may have originated in the high and frigid mountains of Tibet. It was originally used to herd and protect livestock. Massive in size, these magnificent dogs are now considered to be the gentle giants of their ferocious ancestors.

Paired with our giant friend, we have Vietti Castiglione Barolo. For a dog as large as this animal is, we need a wine that is huge on the nose and soft on the palate. Vietti is now on its fourth generation and producing wines in some of the best areas of the region. This was also one of the first wines from Piemonte imported to the United States.

In the 1950s, this winemaker was one of the first to select and vinify grapes from a single vineyard, highlighting the terroir. This wine is almost aggressively expressive on the nose, but when you finally get around to sipping on it, you realize it is actually silky and gentle, much like this giant dog.

Blueberries, orange blossoms, violets, and cherries tease the nose. The palate echoes with rose petals and a deep, brooding earthiness. Wild strawberries, growing hot in the sunlight before being plucked from the vine and popped straight into your mouth with tiny flecks of soil on them, is the best way to describe the lingering finish. I recommend enjoying this wine with spinach puffs while procrastinating paying your bills by playing cards crossed-legged on the floor with your English Mastiff snoozing next to you.

The English Springer Spaniel Is Hardy and Energetic

Prized originally for their muscular, tough stature, English springer spaniels are perfect for keeping in the field all day with their owners. Today they work with K9 units, and they make loving family dogs. Craving company and attention, they are cuddly dogs.

Paired with this loveable dog is Penns Woods Wildflower White. This wine from Pennsylvania, created by Italian winemaker Gino Razzi, is sure to impress the hardest critics. Gino and Davide have been the dream team making these estate wines since 2004.

If you have not yet tried a wine from the area, this is the vineyard worth visiting. With tiny hints of effervescence and the smallest whispers of sugar, this wine is complex and a real crowd-pleaser. Primarily Moscato with Viognier, this wine is almost as cuddly as our spaniel.

It smells like bright, juicy, sweet Honeycrisp apples, honeysuckle flowers in full bloom, and a fresh bouquet of jasmine. The palate is refreshing in its lemon zest and Meyer lemon pith qualities. The long finish is reminiscent of walking through a field of wildflowers with your English springer spaniel trotting along at your heels.

The structure of this wine is reflective of the stature of our spaniel, yet the easygoing, easy-drinking attitudes are complementary. I recommend enjoying this wine with butternut squash and feta tartlets while having a very one-sided discussion with your springer friend about how "just because I went to the bathroom does not mean you can take my spot on the couch."

Fox Terrier

Eleanor & Oliver

The Fox Terrier Is Alert and Lively

As their name implies, the fox terrier was bred for fox hunts in England. Friendly and charismatic dogs, they are independent in nature and good with children, but typically do not play well with other small animals.

Paired with this charming pup, we have Nik Weis St. Urbans-Hof Riesling. The first vines at the property around the St. Urbans-Hof estate buildings were planted by Nik Weis's grandfather in 1949. Many of these parcels have never since been entirely replanted.

The average age of the vines that produce the grapes for the St. Urbans-Hof Estate Riesling is 50 years old. These old vines root deep into the soil, reaching the bedrock of slate, which contains the minerals that give the Riesling its great structure and minerality. Also, the old vines are less vigorous, which results in lower yields but a high ripeness and flavor concentration.

The nose of this wine begins with an enticing aroma of lemon and apple peel, and a whisper of mango and wet stone. On the palate, the wine features a vibrant mouthfeel and great depth of flavor. The finish has some sweetness to it, and the fruit turns a bit more toward grapefruit in the mouth but is balanced with a good amount of minerality. It has a sharp acidity and a lengthy, lingering, lip-smacking finish of sweet and juicy fruit.

This wine is just as charming as the fox terrier, but is not for everyone—especially someone who is not expecting a sweet Riesling—just as our pup does not play well with other small animals. I recommend enjoying the wine with takeout chorizo nachos on a picnic bench while your fox terrier rests its paws on your leg, asking silently for a taste.

The French Bulldog Is Bright and Easygoing

Surprisingly, French bulldogs originated in England. They are an adorable smaller companion dog bred from English bulldogs to accompany workers on trips across the English Channel to France. Easygoing and affectionate, these playful dogs love their family. They are not terribly yappy, but are very alert.

Paired with this companion is Chateau Musar Blanc, a blend of the ancient grape varieties Obaideh and Merwah, indigenous to the mountains of Lebanon and said to be related to Chasselas, Chardonnay, and Semillon. The Hochar family is determined to make their wines as naturally as possible, with minimal human intervention, making them the first organically certified producer in the region.

In their youth, these wines are yellow-gold, subtly oaky, and creamy textured, rich yet dry, and intensely citrusy, with honeyed nuances. Just as easygoing as the Frenchie, the style of this wine has been described as resembling "dry sauternes" or mature white Graves.

It pairs well with a vast array of food. Chateau Musar whites develop tawny hues and mellow spicy characteristics as they age. The winery, 3,000 feet above sea level, is flanked on one side by snow-covered mountains.

The grapes are hand-harvested, wild-yeast-fermented, and made with the bare minimum of sulfur to ensure the wine does not spoil. These wines really are as charming as the French bulldog, and if you were lucky enough to find a large supply of it, you would not tire of drinking this composite of flavor and happiness. I recommend enjoying this wine with French onion dip and Lay's potato chips. Don't forget to pet your Frenchie in between bites; they love the attention.

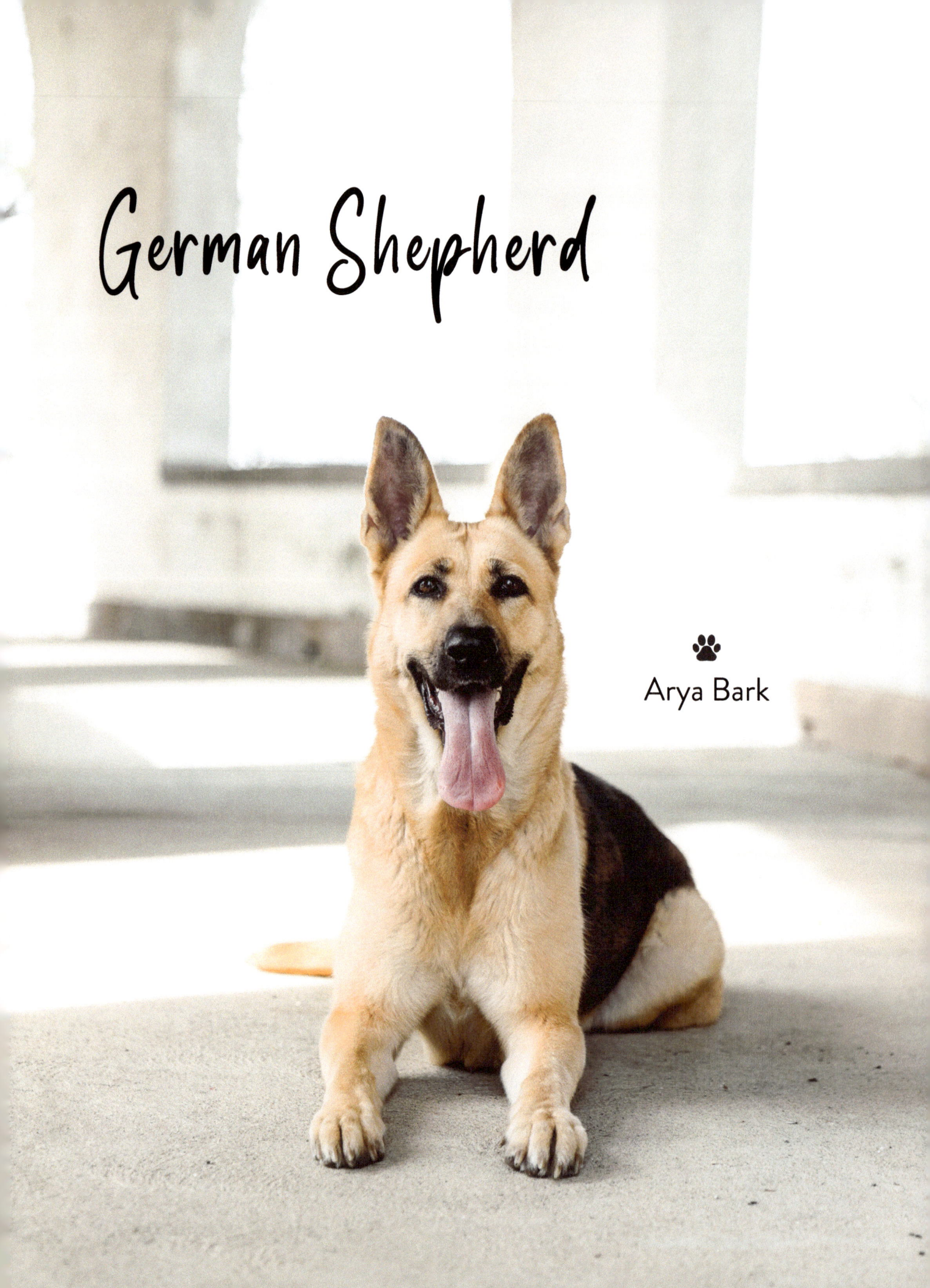

The German Shepherd Is Courageous and Strong

The German shepherd is easily one of the most recognizable dogs today—around the world. Originally designed as shepherds for guarding flocks, they are very strong-willed dogs. They are playful in nature, but can be wary of new people. They will provide a great sense of security for their families.

Paired with this pooch is a wine that is just as easily recognized: Château Haut-Brion. This winery has one of the longest histories of any Bordeaux vineyard. This château is also the only first-growth not located in the Medoc. When the first-growth status was awarded, only four châteaux were awarded this legendary status of quality.

A stunning Bordeaux blend, this wine transcends time in a way a lot of wines strive for, but cannot achieve. Structured in a firm and muscular way, these tannins are supple yet silky. Not aggressive in any fashion, this wine can still pack a punch in its youth.

This revolutionary winery produced one of the first age-worthy wines to come out of the area. They were able to accomplish this by aging longer in oak and topping off their barrels. Havana cigars, chocolate, roasting cedar wood, and fresh leather all resonate on the nose.

The lingering flavor of dried forest floor invokes memories of playing in piles of leaves as a child. You can actually taste the deep beds of gravel that the vines struggle in, with a gorgeous lingering finish of stone and minerality.

This wine is as strong as a German shepherd and just as classic. I recommend enjoying the wine with a grilled salami, pickle, and Swiss cheese sandwich while using your other hand to play tug-of-war with your German shepherd.

German Shorthaired Pointer

Timber

The German Shorthaired Pointer Is Sporty and Affectionate

German shorthaired pointers are versatile hunters and all-purpose gun dogs. Germans in the late nineteenth and early twentieth centuries selectively bred these pups for biddability, with steps taken later to improve stance, style, and nose. They strove to produce the perfect field dog.

Paired with this sturdy pup, we have Numanthia "Numanthia." Hailing from the Toro in Spain, this wine is made from tempranillo grapes. Bodega Numanthia is a living tribute to the fearless warriors of Numancia in Spain, whose inhabitants heroically resisted the Roman army for twenty years in 134 BCE and ultimately preferred to sacrifice their lives rather than surrender.

This single-minded determination is something the German pointer can relate to. The resilience is really evident in the glass. The vineyards grow in the northwest of Spain on clay plateaus and slopes. These remarkable wines are also of historic importance to the Americas, with the wines of the region actually carried on Christopher Columbus's ships in 1492.

Deep purple in color, cranberries, black currant, and violet notes hit the nose immediately. Then, hints of cinnamon, cloves, and black pepper followed by delicate balsamic aromas with mint, eucalyptus, and sandalwood make an appearance on the palate.

This wine is as fearless in flavor as the German pointer is in the field. I recommend enjoying this wine with pretzel bites dipped in melted cheese while you relax in a bubble bath, your German Pointer curled up on the bathmat next to you.

The Golden Retriever Has Great Self-Discipline and a Gentle Spirit

Over the years, the golden retriever has often been used as a gun dog and for retrieving small game like waterfowl. It is one of the most jovial and loyal breeds out there. The golden is the ideal dog for any owner, as they are very adaptable.

Paired with our golden retriever, we have Raveneau Chablis Grand Cru "Valmur." Domaine Francois Raveneau is an extremely difficult to find wine, mostly because their vineyards are made up exclusively of Grand Cru or Premier Cru grapes.

Chardonnay is normally a hard wine to sell to a table of more than three people. Everyone seems to have a strong preference for their preferred style of Chardonnay: either a big, oaky, buttery version, or a lean and crisp Chablis. This Chablis is a home run, and no matter who is at the table, this should be an agreeable compromise.

The wine has some ripe characteristics to it that show warmer tones, as well as a leanness and minerality that really lends something special. With honeysuckle on the nose, citrus notes really come through alongside a slight floral note. Lemon juice, Granny Smith apples, and crushed shells are all prevalent on the palate.

This is a massively adored and highly sought-after wine. Like the golden retriever, it could very easily win a popularity contest or two. The brothers who currently run the show here are the perfect balance of artist and scientist. I recommend enjoying this wine with tuna salad served on rice crackers while taking in the shade under a banana tree as your golden retriever sprawls out in the sun.

The Great Dane Is Highly Adaptable with a Great Attitude

Once called "boar hounds," these dogs have traditionally had their ears cropped to prevent animals from trying to grab at them. They are also considered the world's biggest lap dogs—despite their size, they always try to snuggle on their owners' laps.

Paired with our Great Dane is Biondi Santi Brunello di Montalcino. Franco Biondi Santi is the oenologist at the winery today, carrying on his family name and legacy after more than a century of winemaking.

Brunello di Montalcino is one of the most prestigious Italian red wines out there. It is produced in a very specific area of southern Tuscany with unique features in terms of microclimate, height, and soil type that enable these wines to reach stunning complexity levels. They enjoy truly great balance, expressing both delicacy and fluidity, revealing an inviting bouquet that brings to mind the forest in late spring when the scent of small red-berry fruits meets the floral notes of new shoots on the forest floor, as the earth emanates mineral sensations of fresh moss and aromatic herbs.

It approaches the palate with kindness and softness, leading with notes of red-berry fruits, black cherries, and balsamic that accompany freshness and structure, leading us toward a lengthy finish with firm and angular tannins.

I recommend enjoying this wine with twice-baked potatoes, heavily loaded with bacon, as your Great Dane named Brunello (Bruno for short) barks off in the distance to let the neighbor's dog know he is home.

Great Pyrenees

Falkor

The Great Pyrenees Stands Out from the Crowd

Hailing from the French side of the Pyrenees mountain chain, these dogs were bred to fight off bears, boar, and wolves in the freezing temperatures. Muscular and tough, these stupendous dogs are single-minded in their determination to learn and perform their tasks.

Paired with this sturdy friend, we have Herman Story's Milk & Honey. This big, bold, stunning wine is a blend of tempranillo, grenache, Cabernet Sauvignon, petit verdot, and Syrah. Created by Russell From, this wine is made to stand out, not fit in.

The blend is unusual, but the wine is fierce in its depth of complexity and structure. These grapes are grown in Paso Robles, a wine region that has been gaining in popularity year after year. Luscious and undulating in waves of aromas, the nose offers rich black cherry, toffee, espresso crema, and caramelized beef. The palate is also lush, showing milk chocolate, coffee-cream, roast beef, and root beer flavors.

Wines do not naturally get more muscular than this, which puts it in the same class as our Great Pyrenees. It is high in alcohol and tannins that scream for attention. I recommend enjoying this wine with chocolate-covered pomegranate seeds as you skip rocks over a nearby lake while your Great Pyrenees chases birds.

Greyhound

Sadie & Brienne
(the brindle galgo, or Spanish greyhound)

The Greyhound Is Noble and Fast

Greyhounds were originally bred as hunting dogs in England to chase hare, foxes, and deer. This dog breed can reach speeds between forty and forty-five miles per hour, making them some of the fastest in the dog kingdom. The greyhound is a gentle and sweet-tempered companion with an independent spirit.

Paired with this quick and gentle friend, we have Georges Duboeuf Beaujolais Villages Nouveau from France. Beaujolais nouveau is the first wine released in every year, typically just in time for Thanksgiving, at 12:01 a.m. on the third Thursday in November.

Like our speedy greyhound, this is the fastest wine created and released every year. This producer is the benchmark of all Beaujolais nouveau, as Georges Duboeuf was the first to celebrate the gamay grape's successful harvest with these wines.

As most of their neighbors in Burgundy were making top dollar selling off their Pinot Noirs, Beaujolais was growing the much cheaper gamay grape. They wanted a way to celebrate wine for what it is: a happy beverage that is not to be taken too seriously—just like our greyhound.

Dazzling garnet bordering on purple in color, it is intensely aromatic with succulent notes of red and dark berries. This gamay is immediately expressive and hearty, with a light body dominated by fruitiness that is fresh on the palate. Both our wine and our dog are gentle and loving creatures. I recommend enjoying this wine with grilled branzino, while trying to avoid squeezing lemon on your furry friend.

Havanese

Teddy

The Havanese Is Affectionate and Sassy

Bred in Cuba, the Havanese is also known as the Spanish Silk Poodle. Never put to work, the Havanese have always been lap dogs. Sturdy and social, these dogs tend to think they are much larger than they are.

Paired with our spicy little friend, we have Hermann J. Wiemer HJW Biodynamic Riesling, from one of the top producers in the Finger Lakes region of New York. This was the block used as a trial for biodynamic farming, using vines planted in 2009. The experiment has been a success, and the trial has been rolled out to other blocks in the vineyard.

This is the only combination vineyard, winery, and nursery left in America. This means they grow their own vines from seeds to produce their own grapes and then their own wines, all on their eighty-acre estate on the Western side of Seneca Lake. Wild yeast fermentation really embodies the flavor profile of the region, showcasing the characteristics of the Finger Lakes, including pear, peach, and apricot—funky and wild, just like our little Havanese.

Not bone dry, it has a juicy finish with a touch of sweetness. The mid-palate makes you think of biting into a peach that is so ripe, juice drips down your chin. The minerality on the finish is shocking in its complexity, usually only expected in German wines. I recommend enjoying this wine with spicy pad thai while reassuring your Havanese that they are the only love of your life.

The Irish Setter Is Energetic and Fun-Loving

Bred in Ireland, as the name suggests, this dog was originally a birder, tracking pheasants, geese, and quail over long distances. They are easy to recognize with their deep mahogany or chestnut-colored fur. They are kind in nature and gentle in disposition, but can have a mischievous side.

Paired with our Irish setter, we have Frog's Leap zinfandel. Grown on one of the only dry-farmed vineyards in Napa Valley today, these wines are remarkable in their extraction of flavors.

Luscious aromas of cinnamon and clove entertain the nose. Rich layers of dried cranberries and wild berries give way to plush cherry and jammed boysenberry to delight the palate, while subtle nuances of chestnut and earth never overwhelm.

Perfectly dry and in harmony with the acid, this wine has soft, rounded tannins. It is organically farmed by John Williams, one of the leaders in sustainable farming practices in Napa Valley. An incredible family of winemakers, his son Calder now has his own label as well.

The zinfandel from Frog's Leap is inspired by zinfandels of the past, with petite sirah and Carignane blended in small quantities; even some Napa gamay has found its way into the bottle. This wine is gentle as an Irish setter, but has a firmness and a hint of the game that the dog was bred to capture. I recommend enjoying this wine with duck confit and cranberry mostarda while your gorgeous setter watches out for demented ducks and silly squirrels.

The Jack Russell Terrier Has a Larger-Than-Life Personality

This small dog might have one of the largest personalities of any breed. Originally from the United Kingdom, the Jack Russell terrier was bred to chase foxes. Extremely bold and intelligent but stubborn, they do not like to learn new tricks.

Our Jack Russell terrier is paired with Opus One. A larger-than-life wine created by Robert Mondavi and Baron Philippe de Rothschild, this was one of the first over-the-top wines created in Napa Valley. Opus One Winery sits on the Western portion of Oakville and comprises 100 acres.

The vineyards are always hand-harvested, yet the winemaking process is very modern, using a lot of scientific equipment. Michael Silacci is the current winemaker here; he works to create a highly polished wine that can age for quite a few years. A blend of Cabernet Sauvignon, Cabernet Franc, merlot, petit verdot, and malbec, this is a rich and unctuous wine with a silky palate.

With seductive dark cacao, black cassis, blackberry jam, clove, and nutmeg, it is rounded out with plushy tannins. This wine, like the dog, is extremely bold, and takes some time to calm down in the bottle. I recommend enjoying a glass after at least an hour of decanting, drinking in a cellar while eating a Big Mac with your Jack Russell terrier running around your feet.

The Labrador Retriever Is Outgoing and Well-Balanced

The Labrador retriever is the most popular dog breed in America, year after year. Its history dates back to Newfoundland and Labrador, Canada. One of the friendliest breeds in existence, they make incredible family dogs. Their coats range in color, but their temperaments are similar; they are friendly, affectionate, and high-spirited.

Paired with our Labrador retriever is Far Niente Chardonnay from Napa Valley. These grapes are grown in the Coombsville Vineyards, right in the Vaca Mountains, east of the city of Napa.

Chardonnay is an incredibly versatile grape that grows in many different climates, just like our pooch. A real crowd-pleaser, this wine is often served at higher-end cocktail parties. Bright and refreshing tropical aromatics play on the nose, while melon with hints of fresh fig jump to life on the palate. This chardonnay does not see any malolactic fermentation, so it retains its bright and refreshing acidity. Roasted almonds add a remarkable undertone to this wine, rounding it out to perfection.

Similar to the dog, this wine is rarely disliked and can win over the hardest of critics. Far Niente is the sister winery of Nickel and Nickel, both of which make wines that can last for a long time in your cellar. I recommend enjoying this wine with prosciutto-wrapped cantaloupe while wearing your best Kentucky Derby outfit and sneaking tidbits to your furry friend.

The Maltese Is Bright and Lively

Malta is the area credited for popularizing this beloved and often interbred breed. The Maltese is the oldest toy breed in existence today, dating back at least two millennia. They are friendly and loving and wary of new people, but warm up to them quickly and love attention.

Our Maltese is paired with Azores Wine Company's Arinto dos Açores, grown on a 300,000-year-old island called Pico off the coast of Portugal, where the "soil" is found in ocean fissures amid solidified magma. The vines grow here in wild fashion, creating a unique and delicious flavor profile (like the unique personality of the Maltese).

It is slightly saline, with underripe peach, whispers of apricot, intense minerality, and underlying notes of smoke and acid. It is crisp and refreshing, but serious. This wine, like the Maltese, is easy to fall in love with, but only after an initial warming-up phase (that minerality can be shocking!).

Bright and lively, this is the perfect pairing for our high-spirited little Maltese. If you are lucky enough to find this wine, savor it. I recommend enjoying this on a spring day, tossing some clams into a tin container and then on top of the barbecue with some lemon juice. Don't forget to lavish your attention on your Maltese friend while the clams take their time to open up.

The Papillon Is Regal and Charming

As the name implies (*papillon* is French for "butterfly"), this is a French breed. They are elegant in size and charming in personality. Seriously friendly, these toy pups were prized by royalty.

Not a particularly vocal dog, the papillon tends to be quiet and regal. As this dog is named after a butterfly, we have to enjoy its counterpart in the wine world: Papillon by Orin Swift, a red blend made in Napa Valley, California.

David Swift Phinney fell in love with wine while studying abroad in Italy. He worked at Robert Mondavi Winery in the 1990s as a harvest worker before deciding to open his own cellars. He took the name "Orin" from his father and "Swift" from his mother.

Papillon is a blend of Cabernet Sauvignon, Cabernet Franc, merlot, malbec, and petit verdot. Enjoyed by most heavy red-wine drinkers, this is a real crowd-pleaser, similar to the papillon pup. Smooth and charming, this wine is full of elegant fruit character with oak undertones.

It includes kirsch, blackberry, and black cherry, with an elegant deep-ruby coloring. These cellars are easy to visit in downtown St. Helena, with walk-ins welcome. I recommend enjoying this wine with an RXBAR chocolate sea salt protein bar while playing fetch with your papillon bouncing a tennis ball from your couch.

The Pit Bull Is Agile and Tenacious

*A*s the name implies, these dogs were originally bred to "bait" bulls. The British Isles are where the pit bull started as a farming dog, guarding defenseless animals. For as soft as they are around children, they were later dubbed a "nanny dog." Vastly misunderstood, these dogs are much gentler than their reputation would suggest.

Paired with this pooch is a Billecart Salmon rosé. With a history of more than 200 years in the Mareuil-sur-Ay in Champagne, this vineyard is now on their seventh generation of growers. The estate picks grapes from more than forty crus of champagne across 300 hectares, using only the highest quality grapes in their production.

Subtle and elegant in your glass, this wine oozes aromatics like rose petals, lavender, and juicy raspberries. Tiny effervescence dances softly on your tongue, gentle yet firm.

Like the misunderstood pit bull, this wine is often underestimated and underappreciated. champagne is often used to toast at the start of the meal, then woefully neglected for the rest of it. This wine should be enjoyed throughout your meal, not just as an aperitif. I recommend enjoying it in a coupe glass while munching on original Doritos and playing frisbee-fetch with your friend in the fall.

The Pomeranian Has a Vivacious Personality

German in origin, these tiny dogs have ancestors who were sled dogs. They now come in a much smaller package, with a luxurious coat and tiny fox-like face. They are well known for their yappy ways, and seem to have little-dog syndrome (in which they think they are much larger than they actually are).

Paired with this pup, we have Trefethen merlot. Merlot and Pomeranians seem to have bad reputations, but both of them can be really lovely. Merlot is a wine that also thinks it is much larger than it is.

Smooth and silky, the mouthfeel is normally significantly lighter than the aromas would suggest. Trefethen is a national historic landmark and the only wooden gravity-flow winery in the Napa Valley. With 600 acres of vineyards, it is also one of Napa's largest estate wineries.

They are now on their third generation, and it is very much still a family affair. A deep ruby-red color winks up at you from your glass and introduces a wine with layered aromas of black cherry, blackberry, and baking spice. The palate opens with luscious red fruit, clove, and toasty oak. The finish is all fruit; plushy and fleshy cooked blackberry lingers pleasantly.

The winery is enthusiastic about biodiversity and encourages owls as their solution to field mice and gopher populations. I recommend enjoying this wine with aged cheddar arancini while rolling tiny tennis balls for your Pomeranian, who will ignore them to sit in the sun on their favorite pillow.

The Poodle Is Versatile and Intellectual

Despite what most people seem to think, the poodle originated in Germany. However, they are the national dog of France, which probably contributes to the confusion on the matter. These dogs come in three sizes: standard, miniature, and toy.

Originally used as duck hunters, they have curly hair that protects them from the elements and they are excellent swimmers. Now, because of their desired intelligence and hypoallergenic coat, they are commonly interbred with many other dog breeds.

Paired with our poodle, we have Weingut Richard Böcking rosé from the Mosel in Germany. Established in the early 1600s, this estate boasts what might be the oldest vineyards of Riesling on the Mosel (Ungsberg).

This is a stunning wine made from Pinot Noir grapes. Just as versatile as the poodle, these grapes are made into still, sparkling, red, and rosé, and are blended with other varietals. This particular wine is grown on impossibly steep slopes in Traben-Trarbach, and every once in a while, there is no vintage produced at all when the wild boars eat too many of the grapes.

Underpriced and over-delivered, this bottle will change how you think of German rosé. With luscious raspberry, slate, and soft juicy cranberries, this dry rosé is a thirst-quenching answer to any question. I recommend enjoying this wine at night with freshly caught trout tossed over a fire pit with almonds and butter while your poodle (of any size) stretches out beside you.

The Pug Is Playful and Charming

This flat-faced Chinese dog is well known for its soulful and sad eyes. Another old breed, they were used in ancient China as the refined and preferred pets of high society. They tend to be rather silly and adventurous.

Paired with our pug friend, we have Storm Vrede Pinot Noir from South Africa. Meticulous viticulture, minimal intervention in the cellar, and a constant nod to the Old World instill these wines with a warm personality and character.

With the maiden vintage for two vineyards in 2012, Storm Wines continues to handcraft Pinot Noir from their unique terroirs into very distinctive site-specific wines. This wine has an elegance, showing beautiful balance and length from the natural acidity, which is a faithful depiction of the site's lightly structured decomposed granite soils. Hannes Storm does a remarkable job with both Chardonnay and the finicky Pinot Noir. But with their small production, you should count yourself lucky if you are able to get your hands on more than one bottle per year.

The wine displays layers of dark cherry, berry, and wood spice. As silky smooth as our pug, the tannin structure complements the spicy primary-fruit perfume. Ripe raspberry, lightly crushed rose petals, and freshly picked strawberries all make an appearance on the nose.

The palate confirms these notes, and there is also a deep pomegranate note in the background, with a whisper of cranberry. Soft, supple, silky tannins remind you of the power of Pinot Noir but remain delicate enough for lighter foods. I recommend enjoying this wine with pigs in a blanket while you snuggle with your pug on the sofa watching *The Witcher* on Netflix.

The Rottweiler Is Intelligent and Powerful

The Rottweiler is a large and loyal German breed. It is a top service dog frequently used by police. These dogs are largely misunderstood, as they can be aggressive if trained incorrectly. They require a soft hand during training to retain their calmer temperament.

Paired with this tough canine, we have Dal Forno Romano Valpolicella. This wine consists of traditional indigenous varieties of Corvina, Corvinone, Rondinella, Oseleta, and Croatina.

The estate vineyards and farms are located where the slopes begin to rise toward the mountains, 1,000 feet above sea level. The loose alluvial soils necessitate meticulous vine-pruning (just as our Rottweiler requires meticulous training!), and scrupulous viticultural techniques ensure remarkable grapes.

An incredibly rich and spicy nose of kirsch, sweet cherries, spice box, and hazelnuts is almost aggressive in its assertiveness. Vanilla beans with dried dark-cherry cake and lots of cedar make an appearance on the palate to round out this voluptuous wine. It is full-bodied to the point of bordering on viscous, with perfectly ripe fruit and vibrant acidity. I recommend enjoying this wine on a snowy winter's night with stewed leg of lamb and roasted chestnuts, while your Rottweiler curls up in a fluffy bed nearby.

Saint Bernard

🐾
Gru

The Saint Bernard Is Powerful and Persistent

Swiss in origin, Saint Bernards were working dogs, giant in size, able to survive journeys with humans through the Swiss Alps. In snowy conditions, Saint Bernards were used by monks to find lost travelers. They are often very maternal and love children, as we saw in *Peter Pan* with the "nanny dog."

Paired with this pooch, we have Ciacci Piccolomini Fabius Syrah. Hailing from the Tuscany region of Italy, this wine comes from a practicing organic vineyard. This property actually has wolves living on it, enclosed and taken care of by the owners, the brother and sister team Paolo and Lucia Bianchini, who make fantastic wines sought after throughout the world.

Only 8,000 bottles are made each year. This Syrah tends to show opulent richness and succulence, being compact and linear overall. This wine pulls in opposite directions as it is both firm yet soft, earthy yet fruity, and that's what makes it most interesting.

The bouquet is deeply intense, complex, and persistent. Hints of blueberry, plum, and cherry are enriched and accentuated by elegant spicy notes. The warmth of the grapes shines through; it is soft yet defined in its structure, well balanced and persistent with rounded, angular tannins.

It expresses power, persistence, delicacy, and a character very much in line with our Saint Bernard. I recommend enjoying this wine with confit duck egg rolls, and lots of giant hugs shared with your Saint Bernard.

Schnauzer

Oliver

The Schnauzer Is Smart and Full of Spirit

Schnauzers come in different sizes: standard, miniature, and giant. German in origin, they have been used for many years as guard dogs. If you have smaller rodents around, schnauzers are typically good at clearing them out. Gentle with their families, they make fierce guard dogs.

Paired with this versatile friend is Domaine Pierre Gelin's Chambertin Clos de Bèze. Pierre Gelin is the leading producer in Fixin, Burgundy. Currently on their third generation, Pierre Emmanuel farms organically and tries to impact the environment as little as possible.

Wild-fermented, these wines show their natural flavors and the taste of the land. Pinot Noir can be made still, rosé, or sparkling, as these wines can be as diverse in size and flavor profile as schnauzers can be in temperament.

One of Burgundy's truly great wines, Chambertin Clos de Bèze is said to have been named all the way back in 630 CE. Ripe, fleshy, full-flavored, and intense, the wine tends to have deep color, sturdy but beautifully integrated tannins, and can age for many years in a cool cellar. I recommend enjoying the wine with spicy mushroom jerky while rubbing your schnauzer's pudgy little belly.

Scottish Terrier

Ben & Libby

The Scottish Terrier Is Sturdy and Playful

Another Scottish breed, this guy has been known as the "Scotland Kid." The Scottish terrier is a hypoallergenic breed and a crowd favorite, especially after Jock's appearance in *Lady and the Tramp*. A Scottish terrier has been the "First Dog" in the United States twice now, to presidents Franklin Delano Roosevelt and George W. Bush.

These are fearless little sparky dogs with big voices, and they like to use them. They will chase cats, but generally get along well with other dogs.

Paired with this cutie, we have Turley Estate zinfandel. All their vineyards are either certified organic by California Certified Organic Farmers or are in the process of obtaining organic certification, and they use all natural yeasts in their fermentations. They are some of California's most historic vineyards, producing distinctive wines that reflect their heritage.

This winery focuses on their single-vineyard zinfandels, making them one of the only producers of these terroir-sensitive wines. Similar to the crowd-pleasing Scottish terrier, this wine is dense, powerful, savory, and beloved by the vast majority of people who try it.

Cedar, tobacco, menthol, licorice, and dried lavender flowers create a striking aromatic intensity. I recommend enjoying this wine with grilled teriyaki beef skewers and excessive petting of your Scottish Terrier, as they jump up trying to get your attention.

Shetland Sheepdog

🐾
Sadie

The Shetland Sheepdog Is Affectionate and Powerful

A herd dog originally from the Shetlands in Scotland, the Shetland sheepdog was used in herding sheep, chickens, and ponies. They make excellent watchdogs and are great with children, though they can be aloof with new people.

Paired with our Shetland sheepdog is Fèlsina Chianti Classico Riserva from Tuscany, Italy. The vintners of this winery, a benchmark producer of Chianti, were pioneers of removing the white grapes from their blends and using entirely Sangiovese.

As striking in beauty as the sheepdog, this wine is ruby red with fine tonality and intensity. It has a spicy nose of wild blossoms, warm sun-kissed berries, and mineral tones. Notes of spice and crisp fruit play on the palate, with self-confident but supple tannins and impressive structure.

This wine is absolutely one that will age with grace and dignity, becoming more refined as the years go by. One hundred percent Sangiovese, this grape is beautiful on the nose and palate as well as in the glass with its orange flecks of light. The property where these grapes are grown is charming with its woods, cereal-sown fields, olive groves, ditches and streams, and smaller fields for cultivated and wild herbs as well as medicinal plants, such as alfalfa, sorghum, millet, sunflower, and field beans, all of which contribute to the preservation of biodiversity.

Organically farmed, these grapes come from vines a minimum of thirty years old. I recommend enjoying this wine with tomato and mozzarella bites, eaten off bamboo skewers while prancing through a field of sunflowers, your furry friend chasing rabbits alongside you.

The Shiba Inu Is Daring and Affectionate to Family

The Shiba Inu is Japanese in origin. Somewhat small in stature, this is another ancient breed thought to have originated in the third century BCE. It is still the number one companion dog in Japan. Strong-willed, brave, and daring, they are affectionate with their family but do not care for strangers.

Paired with this beautiful dog is Domaine Huet Vouvray Le Mont Sec. Founded by Gaston Huet in the late 1920s, the vineyard was one of the earliest practitioners of biodynamics. Today, the winery is run and owned by Sarah and Hugo Hwang, an American brother and sister team who strive to maintain the soul of the vineyards.

Verbena tea leaves, juicy pears, oyster shells, and ginger steal the show on this palate. The wine is screaming with minerality, has a twinkle of quince, and is absolutely stunning in the way it comes to life after being open for an hour or more.

This is a wine that many sommeliers appreciate and love, but which those who are not in the know may never think to try. Similar to our stranger-shy pup, this chenin blanc is worth learning to love. Not only is it remarkable in its youth, this vintage also has the structure and finesse to age for years in your cellar. I recommend enjoying this wine with freshly shucked oysters, sitting on a blanket on the beach with your Shiba Inu.

Shih Tzu

Dumble

The Shih Tzu Has a Mind of Its Own

As you can probably guess from the name, the shih tzu originated in China. The name means "lion." A royal dog bred for a life of luxury, shih tzus are friendly, affectionate, and love to be around people. Alert and lively but typically quiet, they are not barkers.

Paired with this regal dog, we have Innate Wine's Jurassic Park Vineyard Chenin Blanc. Grown outside of Los Olivos in Southern California (Santa Ynez AVA), these chenin blanc vines are as old as seventy years in some areas, and completely ungrafted.

This wine has been brought to life by Nathan DeCamps, a native of South Carolina. He tries to keep his style as hands-off as possible, allowing the vines to do what nature intended, similar to how the shih tzu does what it wants regardless of your wishes.

With stunning aromatics on the nose, lifted notes of freshly cut grass and a field of wildflowers waft tantalizingly up at you. The palate is rounded out with clean, crisp minerality, reminiscent of standing close to the sea as the waves crash. Notes of underripe peaches linger for a pleasantly long time. I recommend enjoying this wine with hamachi crudo, pureed avocado, and grapefruit juice while your shih tzu gnaws on a Greenie dental stick right next to your ankles.

The Siberian Husky Is Tough and Cuddly

Russia is the country that bred these popular dogs into existence. Descendants of the original sled dogs, the Siberian husky was used to pull heavy sleds by the Chukchi people of northern Siberia. Known for their ability to maintain their strength on little food, they are muscular and tough yet cuddly and affectionate.

Paired with this majestic breed is Inniskillin Cabernet Franc Icewine. Derek Kontkanen is the brilliant winemaker who creates these hard-to-find works of art. These wines are grown in wineries in Niagara-on-the-Lake, Ontario, British Columbia, and Okanagan Valley.

Solid tannins give structure to this wine, yet are completely in balance with the high acid and sweetness. Not sticky or syrupy, this wine tastes like ripe raspberries, dark cherries, blueberry pie, and espresso beans all rolled into one.

The Cabernet Franc grapes that go into this wine are left on the vine long after all others have been picked, similar to the long-lasting husky's lifespan. I recommend enjoying this wine in the snow with dark-chocolate-covered espresso beans. Just make sure to keep them out of reach of your husky buddy!

Silky Terrier

🐾 Dipper

The Silky Terrier Is Pretty and Energetic

Australian in origin, these long-haired show dogs are quick-footed and high energy. They love to be around their owners and people in general. Incredibly social, they do not like to be alone. It's not in their nature to be particularly yappy, but they will bark with excitement or if they are meeting someone for the first time.

Paired with this pretty dog is István Szepsy Tokaji Dry Furmint from Hungary. Stunning in its complexity and minerality, this wine is remarkable in its youth and gains elegance and dignity as it ages. Bright yellow peaches on the nose, high acid, crisp Granny Smith apples, and the salty sea air fill out a backbone that is unexpected for its grace on the palate. This is a dry expression of the multidimensional variety native to the region.

Brought to life by a legendary winemaker, the grapes for this wine are grown on the Grand Cru hills of Tokaji. At this point in time, these wines are no longer imported to the United States; it might warrant a flight to Budapest to get your hands on some. (Just make sure to also pick up some Unicum Riserva while you are there!)

The wine is as gorgeous as the dog, and as bright and approachable. Shockingly delicious, this wine lingers for a long time after drinking and will leave you craving more. I recommend enjoying a glass with oysters on the half shell, broiled with spinach and hollandaise on top, while you toss the empty shells back into the sea as your silky terrier runs around, chasing seagulls and pigeons.

The Welsh Corgi Is Puppy-Like and Energetic

Wales bred these popular little dogs into existence. The Welsh corgi is short in stature, but not on personality, and has been the preferred dog of the British royal family for centuries. They will act like a puppy for their entire life, never losing steam or energy, making a great family pet.

Paired with our Welsh corgi, we have the Patelin de Tablas Blanc from Tablas Creek Vineyard. This stunning white blend of Rhône varietals brightens a room just by being in it—just like our corgi buddy. The wine incorporates fruit from nine top Rhône vineyards in Paso Robles, each selected for its quality.

Like many white wines from the southern Rhône, this one is based on the crisp acids and rich mouthfeel of grenache blanc, with viognier added for floral and tropical aromatics and small additions of roussanne and marsanne for structure. It is intensely floral on the nose, with notes of honeysuckle, spiced pear, nectarine, and freshly slapped spearmint. In the mouth, it's lush but vibrant with peach pit, Honeycrisp apple, and orange zest flavors, with a salinity on the mid-palate.

Bright acidity softens into creamy richness on the finish, leaving lingering flavors of sweet spice. I recommend enjoying this wine with seared scallops sitting on top of creamy hummus while playing tug-of-war with your corgi's favorite stuffed bunny rabbit toy.

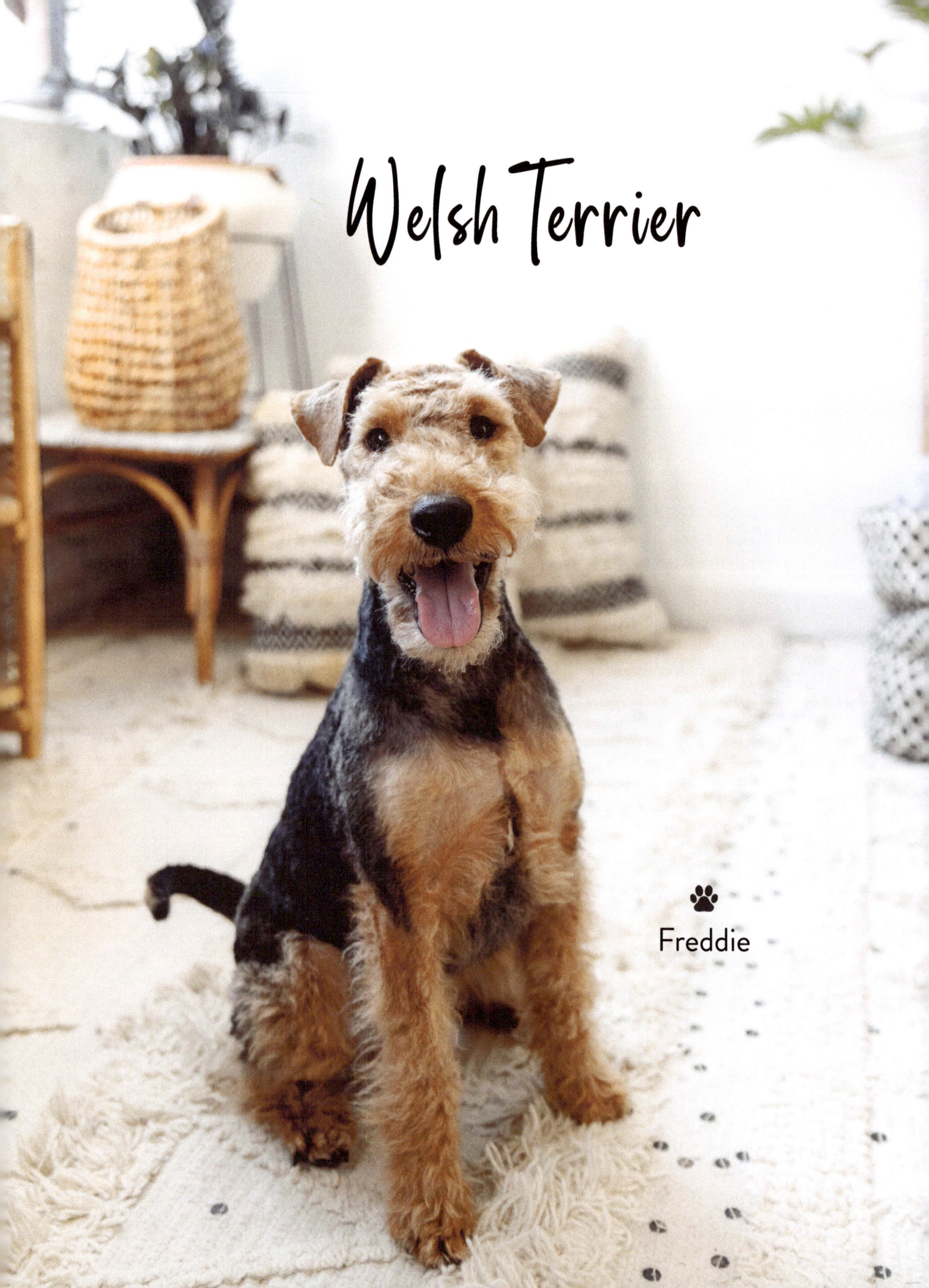

The Welsh Terrier Is Athletic and Energetic

This breed originated in Wales as a small prey hunter—foxes, badgers, and rodents were their original quarry. They are bred for show these days, but are on the UK Kennel Club's list of breeds in danger of dying out. This rare dog is full of energy and will need to be regularly exercised.

Paired with our Welsh Terrier, we have Grande Reserve Naoussa Boutari. Boutari is one of the oldest and most historic wineries in all of Greece, producing some truly remarkable and affordable wines. This one is made from the xinomavro grape, which is indigenous to the area and incredibly hard to find in the US. This vineyard might be singlehandedly responsible for saving this grape varietal, working to plant an abandoned and forgotten piece of history.

Aged for four years before release, this wine will open beautifully in your glass. Dark inky berries, dried forest floor, juicy ripe plums, and a hint of smoke tantalize the nose. A whisper of rosemary, savory herbs, eucalyptus, and cranberries come to life on the palate. The tannins are supple and elegant from age, with a firmness that hints at the longevity of this wine. The lean yet muscular structure echoes our Welsh terrier friend.

Both our Welsh terrier and Grande Reserve Naoussa Boutari are difficult to find, yet completely worth the effort. I recommend enjoying this wine with barbecued portobello mushrooms stuffed with ground beef and sharp Swiss cheese while your Welsh terrier barks loudly at a scurrying woodland creature you can't see.

West Highland Terrier

 Rally

The West Highland Terrier ("Westie") Is Energetic and Fun-Loving

First bred in Scotland, the Westie is the dog used on the label of the Cesar dog food brand. These pups can be possessive of their toys and food, and they need to be socialized early on. They can either be loving and friendly, or appreciate their solitude—this breed has very individualized personalities.

Paired with our finicky friend, we have a hard-to-find wine that is fun and delicious: Weingut Nigl Grüner Veltliner from Austria. The vineyards it comes from are partially located on the hill terraces of the Kremstal, on the fringes of the Bohemian grounds and in a river valley. However, the full vineyards of the estate are spread across different locations.

Wonderfully fresh notes of green, juicy pears mix with a vivid overtone of lemon drop. The palate speaks of crisp freshness, clean-cut peach, subtle yeasty nuance, and fine concentration. This is a lean but wonderfully fresh and bright wine. The finish is all minerality, evoking images of walking along the beach during a storm.

This wine comes in various styles, similar to our Westie. I recommend enjoying a glass with a fried chicken sandwich with extra pickles while you watch your Westie jump through freshly piled leaves.

Yorkshire Terrier

🐾

Riesling

The Yorkshire Terrier Is Tiny and Full of Spunk

The Yorkshire terrier is affectionate and loving but stubborn and mischievous. These are very active dogs, and very alert. Originally bred in the United Kingdom, they were used to chase rats off of docked ships.

Paired with this dog is Trimbach's Clos Ste-Hune from Alsace, France. This is a dry expression of Riesling, rich with succulent aromas and tantalizing fruit character. It is stunningly floral, with minerality and a complex palate that lingers for a long time.

This wine pairs with our Yorkshire terrier because they are both bright, alert, and happy. Activity level, high; acid level, high. You always think these dogs are going to be as sweet as a dessert wine, but they are actually very complex little creatures. Always hand-picked, these dogs do require early hands-on training. Both the wine and the dog have long lives that age with grace and dignity, and might take a few years to calm down from their exuberant and enthusiastic youth.

While not as self-important as this pup, the importance of this wine in the world of great Rieslings is indisputable. I recommend enjoying it with some buffalo chicken wings (blue cheese optional) while your Yorkshire terrier sits next to you on the couch.

Acknowledgments

There are so many people without whom this book would not have been possible.

First and foremost: I would not be where I am today without the love and support of my family. You have always given me all the tools to be successful in this life, and I will be eternally grateful for that fact. I have the most supportive and loving parents, as well as two sisters who are my best friends. My nephews make me laugh, and my brothers-in-law make me feel safe and loved. I am among the luckiest people in the world because of you.

To Zakary Edington, the man who brought me back to life; I had lost all sense of self, all hope, and my soul until you took my hand and gently picked up the pieces of my shattered heart. Thank you for your patience, your kindness, and your unwavering love. Words cannot express how thankful I am for you.

Amanda Jaffe of Love Me Do Photography, you were the best person for this job. Your photos and willingness to work with me made this book; it would not be what it is without you. Carina, thank you for standing in for me a few times. Theresa and Maddie, thank you both for taking a few photos, and thank you for rescuing your dogs as well!

To Richard Kipp, the curator of my favorite museum, The Kipp Collection, for the inspiration and endless stream of ideas. Thank you for the fun and wine.

To my closest friend Rosie: you have been here the longest and have seen me at my best and worst. There are few people as talented as you are, and I hope one day you will see you as I do.

To Hai Tran, Jamie Rubin, Scott Zoccolillo, and Chris Marcus for believing in me when I didn't believe in myself. I would not be the sommelier I am today without all of you. Continue to inspire others the way you did me.

To Mary, for reminding me every day to be happy and have fun; without you my life would have a lot less of both.

To Ross, Brandon, and Austin, my far-away sommelier friends, thank you for never letting distance separate us. Ross, you are the best *Clash of Clans*-mate I could've ever hoped for. Austin, thank you for the endless stream of wine knowledge and for always being my "ti amo." Brandon, thank you for the introduction, and for always trying to do the moral thing.

To my biggest fan Valerie, and her husband Evan, who gave me my start in the world of wine: thank you for the constant push for me to be better and never-ending encouragement.

To Chelsy and Chris, for always being there for me. Tyler, thank you for being my wingman and buddy of Zak.

To Melanie, thank you for listening to my endless drafts and ideas.

To Sydney Grims, for your understanding and kindness. You helped me to plan William's memorial service in a time where I was unsure of which way was up and which way was down. You are a remarkable human, and I am honored to work alongside you.

To Janelle, my faraway friend, I miss you. You inspire me even from afar. Never forget how remarkable you are.

To Allison, for always being there through thick and thin, thank you.

My Fearless Family: you were the most supportive organization I have *ever* had the pleasure of being a part of. I could spend the next twenty pages mentioning you all by name, but I'd have to pay extra for that. Just know: you are all remarkable humans. I am grateful to work with you, and I am proud to be a part of your lives. A special thank-you to Marty, Tamas, Helen, Gabby, Jon, Pete, Lee, Iva, Michelle, Ed, Becca, and Linda.

Alex, Kerrie, and Jaimi: you three are my marketing wizards. I would have a book and no sales without you three. Thank you for all your extra effort to help me. I appreciate you.

To Kayla, Cambria, Shemar, and Andrew, the pieces that Will left behind: I love you.

Len Boris, thank you for bringing me to group therapy on days where I did not want to go. You and your family have been wonderful friends since the day we met.

To Eric, for always using feng shui whenever you come to visit, thank you.

To David, for teaching me how to play blackjack, thank you.

To Michael Weiss, who inspired me to get into wine in the first place, thank you.

To the Philadelphia Sommelier Community: I have always been honored to be among you. Thank you for welcoming me into such a loving and caring support system.

To all of my friends for being the most supporting and loving people, thank you.

To Riesling, my little bundle of joy and constant companion, thank you for not peeing on the rug.

To all of those who have had an impact on my career, there are too many of you to name, but you know who you are, from the bottom of my heart, thank you.

To all of the shelters who helped me to find and photograph your dogs, thank you. Street Tails was incredible in their efforts to make this book happen. The SPCA was also invaluable. Thank you both—I look forward to donating money to you from the sales of this book.

About the Author

Michele Gargiulo is a beverage professional who works in high end restaurants in Philadelphia. She has overseen as many as ten restaurants at a time as the Beverage Director of a large restaurant group. Her experience includes working at luxury hotels as well as many prestigious restaurants. She is a Co-Founder of Energy Drink Ratings, and is passionate about all styles of beverage.

She is a Certified Sommelier from the Court of Master Sommeliers, a WSET Diploma student (currently Advanced), a Certified Sake Advisor from the Sake School of America, an Executive Bourbon Steward from the Stave and Thief Society, and a Certified Specialist of Wine from the Society of Wine Educators. Basically, beverages are her area of expertise. She graduated from The Culinary Institute of America, and prior to that studied Genetics at Rutgers University. She was the Teaching Assistant for the Wines Class at The Culinary Institute of America for a year under Professor Weiss, and has taught wine classes at Montgomery Culinary Institute. She was the beverage director of a small restaurant on the Main Line of Philadelphia for just over four years. The owner founded the American Sommelier Association, and her predecessor was Melissa Monosoff, who is currently one of the few female Master Sommeliers and was also in charge of the Education Department for the Court of Master Sommeliers. She was named one of *Philly Mag*'s New Faces of Wine in 2017, has been written about in a few other magazines, and has done many press appearances on news stations. With over a decade of experience in the field, she is also one of the few females in the industry. She has made her career about making wine more approachable and fun for those who are too intimidated to learn more. She often pairs wine with things that others would not think to, like art, music, feelings, and now, dogs!

Find Michele online at pairingpaws.com or follow her on Instagram at @PairingPawsOfficial.

www.ingramcontent.com/pod-product-compliance
Lightning Source LLC
Chambersburg PA
CBHW041417010526
44107CB00016B/1203